C.H.O.S.E.N.

God Uses Whom He Chooses, God Chooses Whom He Uses

Angie M. R. Gatlin

© 2021
C.H.O.S.E.N.: God *Uses* Whom He Chooses, God *Chooses* Whom He Uses
By: Angie M. R. Gatlin

ISBN: 978-1955127097

Contact the Author: authorangiegatlin@gmail.com
Editor: Anjeanette Alexander
Publisher: Kingdom News Today Publication Services, LLC.

All rights reserved. No portion of this book may be reproduced, stored in a retrieval system, or transmitted in any form or by any means—electronic, mechanical, photocopy, recording, scanning, or other—except for brief quotations in critical reviews or articles, without the prior written permission of the author.

Scriptures have been taken from the Bible Gateway website: www.biblegateway.com

Dictionary definitions were taken from the Merriam-Webster dictionary at https://www.merriam-webster.com/ or Google search results.

Hebrew and Greek lexicon definitions were taken from the *Blue Letter Bible* website: https://www.blueletterbible.org/

Opening quote is an excerpt from Deborah Ann Belka's poem, "Chosen by God" https://www.christart.com/poetry/poem/949

[1] Moore, Beth. (2014). "Identity Declaration." *The LPM Blog*. https://blog.lproof.org/2015/01/identity-declaration.html

[2] Zuck, Roy B. (2009). *The Speaker's Quote Book*. Grand Rapids, MI: Kregel Publications.

[3] Roman Road to Salvation
https://www.christianity.com/wiki/salvation/what-is-the-romans-road-to-salvation.html

[4] Hedrick, Robert. (2021). "Changed by God." *ChristArt*. https://www.christart.com/poetry/poem/6514

[5] Niebuhr, Reinhold. (2018). "Serenity Prayer." https://www.celebraterecovery.com/resources/cr-tools/serenityprayer

[6] Song lyrics from "Raise a Hallelujah" published by The Bethel Music https://bethelmusic.com/chords-and-lyrics/raise-a-hallelujah/

[7] Clarke's Commentary on the Bible. https://www.studylight.org/commentaries/eng/acc/john-16.html

[8] Poem found online https://www.lowell.k12.ma.us/site/handlers/filedownload.ashx?moduleinstanceid=7269&dataid=9829&FileName=Everybody%20Somebody%20Anybody%20Nobody.pdf

[9] Moore, Beth. "Five Statement Pledge of Faith." https://www.pinterest.com/pin/569494315358012290/

[10] Tozer, A. Z. (2020) "God knows instantly and effortlessly." *Tolle Lege*. "Excerpt from *The Knowledge of the Holy* found on a blog post. https://tollelege.net/2020/09/04/god-knows-instantly-and-effortlessly-by-a-w-tozer/

KINGDOM NEWS TODAY
Publication Services, LLC

Dedication

Especially for my parents – James (Daddy) and Geneva (Momma), I love you both so much. Words can't express how proud and how much I count it a privilege to be your little girl (as Daddy always said). My aspiration in life is to be like you guys. You have taught me the importance of integrity, honesty, character and excellent work ethics. For all your diligence, time, attention in reminding me that I could achieve anything, but I had to put the work in. I am truly grateful that you lead me to Christ and give me the roadmap to eternal life. I pray my children will see in me what I see in both of you, my heroes and the wind beneath my wings.

RIL Daddy – December 10, 2014

Especially for My Sister, – Barbara Ann, "aka Bobcat," for all the days and nights that you spent praying with me and for me. All the fasting together, talking and listening to me. I am truly grateful. Your life of courage and determination ministers to me.

Especially for My Brother – Randall Mack "aka Mane," you are the glue for our family. Your compassion, kindness and heart to serve everyone is an example of God's purpose for each of our lives. Your love and care for Mom is to be commended, praise, applauded and admired. What a blessing it is to walk this journey of life with you, my baby brother and my friend.

To my two children by other mothers, my bonus children, Nataisha and Andre. I am grateful for the both of you and how you fill the void of the other two children that I never physically had, but was blessed to get through each of you. You have allowed me to share life with you and I love you guys as if you were my own. And because of you Nataisha I am G.G. Angie, which I am affectionately called by Taylor and Kayla, my bonus grandchildren.

To my three heart beats, my trinity, my gifts from God; Angelo, DeAngelo and Angel. I prayed for you guys and God blessed me above what I could ask or think and gave me the epitome of his creation in three uniquely, compassion, kind hearted children. I prayed through the nine months that I was blessed to carry each of you in my womb and I prayed in the delivery room that the Lord would delivery you into my care. I prayed to be a mother who would help you find your way in this life, but mostly in the life Christ died to give each of you. I am super proud to be your mother, friend and I will never cease praying for the anointing of the Lord to rest, rule and reside over your lives.

And finally, to Charles, the Lord sent you into my life when I was looking for a satisfier, a friend and someone who could walk through life with me. Thank you for being an awesome dad to our children, thank you for being my caregiving husband/Pastor and an amazing housekeeper. Thank you for allowing me to be who God created me to be and supporting me every step of the way. "My Endless Love."

I am thankful for the ministry the Lord has placed in my heart to oversee, *Believing in the Word Ministries*. Our vision is to Grow, Share, and Serve for the transformation of the World for Jesus Christ. We accomplish our vision by making it our mission to intentionally grow our relationship with Jesus Christ by sharing our faith with others and serving God's Church, Community and World.

Forewords

"I do not know why or how Angie chose to walk into my Bible study class in 2001. I do know that I and many others have been immeasurably blessed by her presence, her friendship, her incredible grasp of the Word. You, too, will be blessed, inspired and instructed as you read her book and get to know her heart."

Ann Rice
Psalmist/Teacher
First Baptist Church Pleasant Valley,
Little Rock, AR.

Just when you think your life is ordinary and maybe unnoticed the unthinkable happens. You are suddenly chosen for an assignment by God that may have caught you by surprise. Some assignments you move in silence until permission is given to speak and some are open to talk about it. Lady Angie Gatlin has permission to speak.

Lady Angie Gatlin, a hard worker for the Lord has been Chosen to give insights on how God can choose anybody he wants to by putting the words given by God in a book. She will definitely inspire us to be more open about allowing God to use us in his way. She is qualified for this assignment because of her dedication to God. She is always allowing God to give her knowledge to teach others. God has used this beautiful lady to go tell people their assignments. I am one of those people chosen by God to write about my friend. It is an honor to encourage people to read this book to elevate our thinking to a higher level.

Tina Allen
The Connected Chosen People Ministry,
Little Rock, AR

Angie Gatlin is a gifted writer and communicator. Her words will open up your heart to new hope, hope that is found in Christ alone. The collection of thoughts and reflections contained in this book will help all of us to navigate life's trying and confusing moments with a basis in scripture. This gathering of stories confirms to us that God's fingerprints are everywhere.

Kim Smith
Friend/Co Worker/Christ the King Church

We have had the pleasure of experiencing a loving, Godly Mother since birth. Her drive and dedication have always been apparent in her advocacy for Christ and her late-night study sessions. For many years we have watched as people admired her knowledge and memory of the Bible and her profound speaking and preaching, while we also looked up to her work ethic and perseverance. This book is a remarkable accomplishment and timely coming from an exceptional value-driven woman that we have the honor of calling "Mom."

Your Seeds,
Angelo, DeAngelo and Angel

*"According as he hath chosen us in him
before the foundation of the world,
that we should be holy and without blame
before him in love: Having predestinated us
unto the adoption of children by Jesus Christ to himself,
according to the good pleasure of his will,
To the praise of the glory of his grace,
wherein he hath made us accepted in the beloved."*

Ephesians 1:4-6 (KJV)

We are chosen by God,
handpicked for His vine
to serve and worship Him
to bring Him glory divine.

Excerpt from "Chosen by God"
by Deborah Ann Belka

Table of Contents

Preface 1

Introduction Why Did God Choose ME? 7

Chapter 1 – **C** – Chosen to Change 13

Chapter 2 – **H** – Chosen to say Hallelujah 25

Chapter 3 – **O** – Chosen to Overcome 39

Chapter 4 – **S** – Chosen to Serve........................... 51

Chapter 5 – **E** – Chosen to Endure 65

Chapter 6 – **N** – Chosen to Never Quit................... 75

Conclusion – Crossing the Finish Line 89

Preface

The Word of the Lord responds to the assignment of being chosen in this way:

> Psalm 68:11 (KJV): *"The Lord gave the word: great was the company of those that published it."*
>
> Psalm 68:11 (NET): *"The Lord speaks; many, many women spread the good news."*

Angie Gatlin responds this way . . .

> Isaiah 50:4 (TLB): *"The Lord God has given me his words of wisdom that I may know what I should say to all these weary ones. Morning by morning he wakens me and opens my understanding to his will."*

I praise Jehovah that I am only one of the chosen W.O.G. – Women of God.

Beth Moore called us Women of God with her Identity Declaration[1]:

C.H.O.S.E.N.

- I am a W.O.G. (Woman of God)
- Redeemed by Jesus Christ
- Loved, Pursued, and CHOSEN
- Equipped with Words of Life
- Clothed in Strength and Dignity
- Commissioned Here and Now
- Gifted by the Spirit
- Forgiven and Unbound
- Blessed is She Who Believed.

I want to focus the biblical spotlight on the absolute necessity of glorifying God by providing purposeful "rhema word" that will lift up and encourage the body of Christ because I love HIM. *Rhema* in the Greek means "utterance" or "thing said" or the spoken word of God. I have read many books, but the Bible reads me. The Bible doesn't need to be rewritten, but it needs to be reread.

According to Joshua 1:8 (KJV), it should be reread daily: *"This book of the law shall not depart out of thy mouth; but thou shalt meditate therein day and night, that thou mayest observe to do according to all that is written therein: for then thou shalt make thy way prosperous, and then thou shalt have good success."*

In my own provocative way, with the aid of the Holy Ghost, I have written this book because I am just like you…God saw the best in me when no one else did.
It is now clear to me that although I was not searching for God, He was searching for me. John 15:16 (NIV) says, *"You did not choose me, but I chose YOU."* The King James Version says, *"Ye have not chosen me, but*

Angie M. R. Gatlin

I have chosen you." The Bible teaches that long before you and I were ever conceived in our mother's wombs, God already knew us and was calling us to be His children with a special, peculiar purpose to fulfill in this world. He confirms this in His Word:

> Jeremiah 1:5 (NIV): *"Before I formed you in the womb I knew you, before you were born I set you apart; I appointed you as a prophet to the nations."*
>
> Isaiah 49:1 (NAS): *"Listen to Me, O islands, and pay attention, you peoples from afar. The LORD called me from the womb; from the body of my mother, he named me."*
>
> Isaiah 43:10 (KJV): *"Ye are my witnesses, saith the LORD, and my servant whom I have chosen: that ye may know and believe me, and understand that I am he: before me there was no God formed, neither shall there be after me."*

But my life is worth nothing to me unless I use it for finishing the work assigned me by the Lord Jesus – the work of telling others the Good news about the wonderful grace of God (Acts 20:24 (NLT). It is His story that I get to tell for His glory. In other words, Angie Marie Roberts Gatlin is a nobody trying to tell everybody about somebody who can save anybody.

I grew up in Monroe County – a little town called Clarendon, Arkansas in the Delta Region with a population around 2, 500. One of our favorite pastimes was shooting basketball on a pole with a bicycle rim nailed to it, which served as the basketball hoop. I lived in the part of town called New Addition. The basketball court, respectfully known as the meeting place or hang out, was directly in front of my house.

On an average day, the children in the neighborhood would gather to play basketball. We would choose two leaders. The leaders would choose players to be on their individual teams, while the rest of the kids would lift their hands or show obvious signs that they wanted to be chosen. Those children who were not chosen were left with regret and disappointing faces that expressed their thoughts and feelings.

These children were left with questions of why: why I'm not good enough, why I'm not coordinated enough, why I'm not talented or adequate enough, or why I'm not skilled enough to be chosen. Someone would even say I've never been chosen for anything in my life!

If you have ever felt that way, then you are in good company because this book is for you.

Now I say: "You are Chosen! I am Chosen! This I believe, this I trust!"

This book is stimulating, entertaining, interesting, fascinating, and challenging. It goes right to the heart of the matter where the rubber meets the road and speaks to us in a language that we can all understand and apply.

That language is the very breath of God: The Word, the Logos, the written word of God.

Angie M. R. Gatlin

Before we begin our journey, let's reflect on three perspectives of God's Word: biblical, theological, and of course, your personal views.

FROM A BIBLICAL PERSPECTIVE

Isaiah 55:11 (KJV): "So shall my word be that goeth forth out of my mouth: it shall not return unto me void, but it shall accomplish that which I please, and it shall prosper in the thing whereto I sent it."

2 Timothy 2:15 (KJV): "Study to shew thyself approved unto God, a workman that needeth not be ashamed, rightly dividing the word of truth."

2 Timothy 3:16&17 (KJV): "All scripture is given by the inspiration of God, and is profitable for doctrine, for reproof, for correction, for instruction in righteousness: That the man of God may be perfect, thoroughly furnished unto all good works."

Psalm 119:105 (NLT): "Your word is a lamp to guide my feet and a light to my path."

Hebrew 4:12 (KJV): "For the word of God is quick, and powerful, and sharper, than any two-edged sword, piercing even to the dividing asunder of soul and spirit and of the joints and marrow, and is a discerner of the thoughts and intents of heart."

C.H.O.S.E.N.

FROM A THEOLOGICAL PERSPECTIVE

"It is the mind of God, the state of man, the way of salvation, the doom of sinners, the happiness of believers, light to direct you, food to support you and comfort to cheer you." – Roy B. Zuck (2009), *The Speaker's Quote Book*[2]

"It's doctrines are holy, It's precepts are binding, It's histories are true, It's decisions are immutable, Christ is it's grand subject. Our good it's design and the glory of God it's end." – Roy B. Zuck (2009), *The Speaker's Quote Book*[2]

"Read it to be wise. Believe it to be safe. Practice it to be holy. It should fill the memory, rule the heart, and guide the feet." – Roy B. Zuck (2009), *The Speaker's Quote Book*[2]

"It is the traveler's map, the pilgrim's staff, the pilot's compass, the soldier's sword, the Christian's charter, a mine of wealth, a paradise of glory, a river of treasure." – Roy B. Zuck (2009), *The Speaker's Quote Book*[2]

FROM YOUR PERSPECTIVE

Reflect on what you have just read. What are your thoughts about the power of the written Word of God?

Introduction

WHY DID GOD CHOOSE ME?

When you are chosen by God, it is:

> *Distinct*, and you can't deny it.
> *Priceless*, and you can't purchase it.
> *Authentic*, and it can't be duplicated or imitated.
> *Official*, and no one can stop or block it.
> *Real*, and it can't be denounced or condemned.
> *Serious*, and it can't be avoided.
> *Plain*, and you can't misunderstand it.
> *Personal*, and you can't overlook it.

When you are chosen by God, He has stamped His approval on you, and it is signed, sealed, delivered and *you are His*!

Sometimes, when you are chosen by God, you may be still thinking: But *why* did He choose *me*?

Over and over again, I have asked this very question. I have pondered in my heart: Why would the Master of the Universe select someone like me?

C.H.O.S.E.N.

Over and over again, I have contemplated why God would choose a brown-eyed, freckled face, tiny voice girl (like me) to share His gospel.

I have come to learn and know that Isaiah 55:8 (NIV) is correct, *"For my thoughts are not your thoughts, neither are your ways my ways."* The New Living Translation explains it this way, "My thoughts are nothing like your thoughts, says the Lord. And my ways are far beyond anything you could imagine."

I'm so glad that God is not concerned with things such as appearance, power, or ability, but He is concerned with our availability. Often the person whom God chooses doesn't meet man's requirements, fulfill man's expectations, or receive man's approval; they are not prepared, popular or well known. God makes no mistakes in His selections, and He does not apologize for them. He makes no excuses for using whom He chooses and choosing whom He uses.

John 15:16 (NIV) says, *"You did not choose me, but I chose you and appointed you, so that you might go and bear fruit – fruit that will last – and so that whatever you ask in my name the Father will give you."*

When God chooses you and me, He chooses people that the world chooses last. He actually prefers to choose the weak instead of the strong. God loves saving the uneducated, the foolish, the addicted, the broken, the downcast, and the imprisoned; in short, He specializes in choosing those who are stained, stagnated, and stuck in their stuff, and those the world has counted as nothing and unimportant.

Angie M. R. Gatlin

In the New Testament, *chosen* is almost always a translation of the Greek word, *eklektos*, (Strong's #1588), which literally means "to pick out, to choose, to select for oneself." The Hebrew meaning of *chosen* is a noun (*bakhir/vakhir*) (Strong's 972) and comes out of the verb *bakhlar*. It has a significant footprint in scripture as being elected.

Merriam-Webster defines *chosen* as a noun which means "one who is the object of choice or of divine favor: an elect person." As an adjective, it means "to be selected or marked for favor or special privilege."

I believe that Deuteronomy 7:6 (KJV) illustrates what it means to be chosen: *"For thou are an holy people unto the Lord thy God: the Lord thy God hath chosen thee to be a special people unto himself, above all people that are upon the face of the earth."*

The key issue is who chooses and who is CHOSEN. God doesn't require a job interview or an application. God doesn't require a resume, portfolio, or degree. God doesn't hire, fire, or lay off like the world's employment. God doesn't ask us to get right before we come to Him, but He takes us in, right where we are. God has chosen all sinners. As we have often heard, we are sinners saved by grace.

God loves the sinner but hates the sin: those with popular and unpopular sins, those with social and secret sins, those with public and private sins, those with past and future sins, those with daytime sins and nighttime sins, those with corporate and individual sins, those with direct and indirect sins, and those with intentional and ruthless sins. There are many reasons why God shouldn't have looked through the crowd or pulled open the curtains of Heaven and chosen us.

The Apostle Paul records that we all travel the Roman Road. The Roman Road to Salvation is a selection of Bible verses taken from the book of Romans that present the plan of salvation through faith in Jesus Christ.
Come walk the Roman Road[3] with me:

- Romans 3:23 (NKJV): *"For all have sinned and fall short of the glory of God."*

- Romans 3:10 (NKJV): As it is written: *"There is none righteous, no, not one."*

- Romans 6:23 (NKJV): *"For the wages of sin (is) death, but the gift of God (is) eternal life in Christ Jesus our Lord."*

- Romans 5:8 (NKJV): *"But God demonstrates His own love toward us, in that while we were still sinners, Christ died for us."*

- Romans 10:9-10 (NKJV): *"If you confess with your mouth the Lord Jesus and believe I your heart that God has raised Him from the dead, you will be saved. For with the heart one believes unto righteousness, and with the mouth confession is made unto salvation."*

- The final aspect of the Romans Road for the chosen's salvation is the results of salvation. Roman 5:1 (ESV) has this wonderful message: *"Therefore, since we have been justified by faith, we have peace with God through our Lord Jesus Christ."*

Angie M. R. Gatlin

After walking the Roman Road, the questions still ring loud and clear. Let's look at each one and compare the way we respond to the way God answers.

Why, O Why, Did God Choose Me?
I'm weak, fragile, and confused.
I'm a loser. I'm worthless.
I'm so disorganized and dysfunctional.
I can't get my act together.
I can't get on track and stay on track.
I don't dot all my I's, cross my t's, and fill in every blank.

Why Did God Choose Me?
My private life is a failure.
My public life is complicated.
Mu inner life is a mess.
My social life is dead.
My emotional life is in a disarray.
My physical life is unhealthy.
My personal life is unbalanced.
My career life is unsuccessful.
My spiritual life is as filthy rags.
My mental life is full of depression and anxiety.

Why Did God Choose Me?
I'm a splendid, successful sinner.
I'm a lovable, lazy loser.
I'm a miserable misfit.
I'm a fantastic failure.
I'm a reliable rebellion.
I'm a lousy liar.
I'm a carnal Christian.

C.H.O.S.E.N.

Why Did God Choose Me?
I'm a wondering Woman.
I'm a fussing Wife.
I'm an unreliable Mother.
I'm an unfaithful Servant.
I'm an undedicated Missionary.
I'm a slothful Evangelist.

Here Are God's Answers To The Questions…
We look at our outward, but God looks at the inward.
We value popularity, but God values character.
We look at intelligence, but God searches the heart.
We look at our money, but God honors our integrity.
We talk about what we own, but God talks about what we give away.
We boast about whom we know, but God notices whom we serve.
We list our accomplishments, but God looks for a humble spirit.
We value education, but God values wisdom and understanding.
We love sizes, but God notice quality.

"It is not the quantity, but the quality." – Pastor Gatlin

We live for fame, but God examines our motives.
Our views are shallow, but God's views are deep.
Our view is temporary, but God's view is eternal.

Now let us discuss what each letter of the word CHOSEN means. As you are reading each chapter write your thoughts in the journal section after each chapter. Be sure to note your personal changes.

Chapter 1

CHOSEN TO CHANGE

Roman 12:2(NIV): *"Don't copy the behavior and customs of this world, but let God transform you into a new person by changing the way you think. Then you will learn to know God's will for you, which is good and pleasing and perfect."*

Isaiah 43:19(ESV): *"Remember not the former things, nor consider the things of old. Behold, I am doing a new thing, now it springs forth, do not perceive it? I will make a way in the wilderness and rivers in the desert."*

C.H.O.S.E.N.

1 Peter 2:9 (NIV): *"But you are a chosen people, a royal priesthood, a holy nation, God's special possession, that you may declare the praises of him who called you out of darkness into his wonderful light."*

My Affirmation

I (YOUR NAME) have been Chosen to Change.

What Exactly Does It Mean To Be Chosen To Change?

The word *change* in the Greek language is *metanoe'o*, according to the Strong Concordance (#3340). It means to change one's mind or purpose. Metanoe'o represents a person's decision to change the direction of his or her life based upon the perception of the truth given by the Holy Spirit. Only the Holy Spirit has the power to make the changes God wants to make in our lives.

In Philippians 2:13 (NLT), *"Paul explains that God is working in you to give you the desire and the power to do what pleases Him. The Holy Spirit not only transforms us into a new creation by entering into us, but He also changes us by bringing us into an intimate relationship with God."*

Some scholars believe that it means to repent or change the inner man. A time for change is when God has convicted us that we need to change! It is time to stop procrastinating and to do what it takes to change (2 Corinthians 6:2b KJV).

Don't you wish change was easy? Even Leo Tolstoy mentions that it is not fun. I have found that most people do not desire real change until they reach the bottom. We often say that we want to change. We may even try to change ourselves. We say things like, "I am going to turn over a new leaf. I am going to try harder. I am going to pull myself up by my bootstraps. I am going to get my life out of the ditch. Things will be different this time, you wait and see." But ultimately, our best-intentional attempts at change are fleeting and unsuccessful.

We must be willing to view change from a different perspective and adopt a new attitude. For example, Sean Higgins, a former basketball player said, "Every day the clock resets. Your wins don't matter. Your failures don't matter. Don't stress on what was, fight for what could be." The late poet, Maya Angelou said, "If you don't like something, change it. If you can't change it. Change your attitude."

Perhaps Paul best explains the process of change in Ephesians 4:22-24 (NIV): *"You were taught, with regard to your former way of life, to put off your old self, which is being corrupted by its deceitful desires; to be made new in the attitude of your minds; and to put on the new self, created to be like God in true righteousness and holiness."*

Here's a clear definition of chosen to change in two different acrostic forms:

C.H.O.S.E.N.

C – Change is hard, but rewarding
H – Humility makes it easier
A – All adventures test our courage
N – Not wanting it, we stay on life's roller-coaster
G – Getting off of it, we need to take risks
E – "Every breath is a new challenge of our beliefs."

C – Concentrate on a new outcome
H – Have a vision of what you want to achieve
A – Always be open to the new possibilities
N – Never let fear dictate your decisions
G – Give your new direction a chance to work
E – "Embrace the change as it unfolds."   Dan Mount

The idea of being chosen to change sounds good, but when we get down to it, it actually means living different. Change is a lifelong process of renewal. You should be able to see the distinct difference between the old person that you were and the new person that you are in Christ Jesus.

These days, the idea of "necessary change" is not popular. There are many who want to claim Christianity without having to actually live a Christ-like lifestyle. You should be able to sing like the old country preachers. . . "I ain't what I should be, but I thank God I ain't what I used to be."

The late American Gospel singer, musician and composer, Rev. James Cleveland performed a song that describes the process of change. He said, "If you see me and I'm not walking right. If you hear me and I'm not talking tight. Remember God is not through with me yet – Please Be Patient with Me. God Is Not Through With

Angie M. R. Gatlin

Me Yet [PBPWMGINTWMY]! But when God gets through with me, I shall come forth as pure gold."

It's not enough to just claim to believe or say that you're a Christian. There has to be a change. There should be evidence in your life that you truly follow Jesus. You have to be transformed. The great news is that Jesus is in the transformation business…

Hallelujah!

This means that those who are chosen for change, you and I, will undergo a complete transformation. This transformation is a miraculous work of God that's done on the inside as it begins to reveal a steady changing of behavior on the outside.

You see that God of ours loves us where we are, but He loves us too much to leave us where we are. God will come all the way from where He is just to get you and me to where He needs us to be. This reminds me of the process that a caterpillar goes through to become a butterfly. An excerpt from Robert Hedrick's poem[4], "Changed by God," describes it best:

> As He changed the caterpillar's looks,
> so can He change man's heart,
> By lifting him out of the sinking sea
> of sin into a brand, new start.
> His appearance will not likely change,
> yet a difference should be seen,
> this'll be the presence of God giving
> his light a much brighter beam.

C.H.O.S.E.N.

Strong's Concordance also records two other Greek words that connect to chosen to change:

> *Emiotpe*: to turn to; to be converted
> (Strong #1994; 2 Chronicles 7:14 NIV).
>
> *Meta*: to regret or to be sorry
> (Strong #3338; Psalm 38:18 ESV).

In Philippians 3:13-15 (ESV), Paul states, *"Brothers, I do not consider that I have made it my own. But one thing I do: forgetting what lies behind and straining forward to what lies ahead, I press on toward the goal for the prize of the upward call of God in Christ Jesus."*

Let the prize of the upward call of God in Christ Jesus motivate us to change. Let those of us who are mature think this way, and if in anything you think otherwise, God will reveal that also to you.

Think of the Old Testament story recorded in Genesis 32:22-32 about Jacob wrestling with the angel of the Lord. He came away with a permanent limp and a new name – he was a different man. Goodbye to Jacob, the shyster; hello to Israel, the man who prevails with God.

In the New Testament, there is a very familiar story recorded in Acts 9 about a man named Saul, hell bent on destroying Christians. Saul had an encounter with Jesus on the road to Damascus that literally knocked him on his knees and blinded him. He came away from that experience as a new man, totally transformed. Goodbye to Saul the terrorist; hello to Paul the apostle.

Angie M. R. Gatlin

Now look at Angie Gatlin's story. I describe my story like the songwriter, James Rowe, writes in the 1912 gospel hymn, "Love Lifted Me":

> I was sinking deep in sin, far from the peaceful shore, Very deeply stained within, Sinking to rise no more, But the Master of the sea heard my despairing cry, from the waters lifted me – now safe am I. Love lifted me, when nothing else could help, love lifted me.
>
> All my heart to him I give, even to him I'll cling, in his blessed presence live, ever his praises sing. Love so mighty my soul's best songs; faithful, loving service, too, to him belongs. Love lifted me, when nothing else could help, love lifted me.

Now he gets the glory out of Angie Gatlin's life, and I get to tell His story. I'm just a nobody trying to tell everybody about somebody who can save anybody. I have come a long way from the time that I allowed God to come into my life and take away my sins and to begin the transformation of my life into what He desires of me. I must admit that I still have a long way to go, but the good news is that God never stops loving me and changing me with His gentle touch from glory to glory.

In 2 Corinthians 3:18 (NIV), Paul states, *"And we, who with unveiled faces all reflect the Lord's glory, are being transformed into his likeness with ever-increasing glory, which comes from the Lord, who is the Spirit."* The King James Bible says, "Being transformed from glory to glory."

C.H.O.S.E.N.

Those who are chosen to change understand three profound statements that I trust and believe:

1. God didn't give us new hands, but they do new things.

2. God didn't give us new feet, but they go new places.

3. God didn't give us a new mouth, but it says new words.

Socrates, the great Greek philosopher from Athens, said, "The secret of change is to focus all of your energy, not on fighting the old, but on building the new." Niebuhr's Serenity Prayer[5] gives us a way to do this:

> God grant me the serenity to accept the things I cannot change; courage to change the things I can; and wisdom to know the difference. Living one day at a time; Enjoying one moment at a time; accepting hardships as the pathway to peace; taking, as He did, this sinful world as it is, not as I would have it; trusting that He will make all things right If I surrender to His will; so that I may be reasonably happy in this life. And supremely happy with Him forever and ever in the next. Amen.

History tells us that God has always called His chosen people to decide between Heaven and Hell: a choice between life or death, a choice to decide where you will spend eternity. The Apostle Paul explains it best in 1

Corinthians 5:17 (KJV): *"Therefore; if any man be in Christ, he is a new creature: old things are passed away; behold all things are become new."*

When you are chosen to change, there will be many changes and adjustments from worldly to heavenly in your life:

- Relationships will change.
  2 Corinthians 6:14 (NIV): *"Do not be yoked together with unbelievers. For what do righteousness and wickedness have in common? Or what fellowship can light have with darkness?"*

- Activities will change.
  Hebrew 10:25 (KJV): *"Not forsaking the assembling of ourselves together, as the manner of some is; but exhorting one another: and so much the more, as you see the day approaching."*

- Values will change.
  Mark 8:36 (KJV): *"For what shall it profit a man, if he shall gain the whole world, and lose his own soul?"*

- Interests will change.
  Colossians 3:2 (KJV): *"Set your affections on things above, not on things on the earth."*

- *Purposes will change.*
  Matthew 6:33 (NIV): *"But seek first his kingdom and his righteousness, and all these things will be given to you as well."*

C.H.O.S.E.N.

I am chosen to CHANGE!

Angie M. R. Gatlin

C.H.O.S.E.N.

Chapter 2

H

CHOSEN TO SAY HALLELUJAH

Revelation 19:1 (NIV): *"After this I heard what sounded like the roar of a great multitude in Heaven shouting: Hallelujah! Salvation and glory and power belong to our God."*

Psalm 146:1 (ESV): *"Praise the Lord! Praise the Lord, O my soul!"*

C.H.O.S.E.N.

Ephesians 5:20 (ASV): *"Always giving thanks for all things in the name of our Lord Jesus Christ to God, even the Father."*

1 Thessalonians 5:18 (NASB): *"In everything give thanks for this is God's will for you in Christ Jesus."*

My Affirmation

I (YOUR NAME) Have Been Chosen to Say Hallelujah.

What Exactly Does It Mean To Be Chosen To Say Hallelujah?

The word *hallelujah* in the Greek language is *hall'elouia*, which means "Praise the LORD." If we have been chosen to say Hallelujah, it would be good to know what we have been chosen to do. Hallelujah consists of two words. *Hallel* means to praise, to boast in, to shine forth to be worthy of praise, and/or to be commended." *Jah* is a shortened form of "Jehovah," which means "the self-existent and eternal one." He who will be, who is and who was.

The name Jehovah is an English translation of the Hebrew name of God – the four letters (YHWH), known as the Tetragrammaton. Jehovah appears several times in the King James Version in the Old Testament; some are the actual names with Jehovah attached, and others explain what the Lord does and how He does it.

Angie M. R. Gatlin

1. *Jehovah Medoddishkem – The Lord who sanctifies – Exodus 31:13 (KJV):* "Speak also to the children of Israel, saying, Verily my Sabbaths ye shall keep, for it is a sign between me and you throughout your generations, that ye may know that I am the Lord that doth sanctify you."

2. *Jehovah Tsidkenu – The Lord our righteousness – Jeremiah 33:16 (KJV): "In those days shall Judah be saved, and Jerusalem shall dwell safely: and this is the name where with she shall be called, The Lord our righteousness."*

3. *Jehovah El Roi – The God who sees me – Genesis 16:13 (KJV): "And she called the name of the Lord that spake unto her, Thou God seest me: for she said, Have I also here looked after him that seeth me?"*

4. *Jehovah Rapha – The Lord that healeth – Exodus 15:26 (KJV): "And said, If thou wilt diligently hearken to the voice of the Lord thy God, and wilt do that which is right in his sight, and wilt give ear to his commandments, and keep all his statutes, I will put none of these diseases upon thee, which I have brought upon the Egyptians: for I am the Lord that healeth thee."*

5. *Jehovah Shalom – The Lord our peace – Judges 6:24 (KJV): "Then Gideon built an altar there unto the Lord, and called it*

C.H.O.S.E.N.

Jehovah shalom: unto this day it is yet in Ophrah of the Abiezrites."

6. *Jehovah Jireh – The Lord will provide – Genesis 22:14 (KJV): "And Abraham called the name of that place Jehovah Jireh; as it is said to this day, In the mount of the Lord it shall be seen."*

7. *Jehovah Nissi – The Lord our Banner – Psalm 20:5 (KJV): "We will rejoice in thy salvation, and in the name of our God we will set up our banners: the Lord fulfil all thy petitions."*

8. *Jehovah Ra'ah – The Lord our Shepherd – Psalm 23:1 (KJV): "The Lord is my shepherd; I shall not want. He maketh me to lie down in green pastures: he leadeth me beside the still waters. He restoreth my soul: he leadeth me in the paths of righteousness for his name's sake."*

9. *Jehovah Shammah – the Lord is Present – Psalm 16:11(KJV): "You will show me the path of life; in your presence is fullness of joy; at your right hand are pleasures forevermore."*

As our Savior and Redeemer, Jesus Christ operates with mighty power in each and every one of these offices of salvation and redemption. He is the Lord who never leaves us and never fails us. Hallelujah!

Each week, around the world, thousands of Christians congregation raise their voices in worship with 24 powerful profound words. These 24 words are commonly known as "The Doxology" written by Thomas Ken in 1674. He was an Anglican priest, hymn writer, bishop and the royal chaplain to Charles II of England. It goes like this: "Praise God from whom all blessings flow, Praise Him, all creatures here below; Praise Him above, ye Heavenly host; Praise Father, Son and Holy Ghost."

I think most members of the body of Christ who have been chosen to say hallelujah have learned how to say "hallelujah anyhow." We don't say hallelujah because of; we say hallelujah in spite of. We don't say hallelujah just on good days, but on bad days; we don't just say hallelujah on the mountain, but we say it in the valleys also.

Being chosen to say hallelujah is our proclamation of confidence to the One who sits high but has the ability to see down low. We, the chosen, shout hallelujah because we recognize that even though it may appear that our burdens are overbearing, we understand what Paul left on record in Ephesians 3:20 (KJV): *"Now unto him that is able to do exceeding abundantly above all we ask or think, according to the power that worketh in us".*

Paul also left on record 2 Corinthians 12:9b (NIV): *"My grace is sufficient for you, for my power is made perfect in weakness."*

We who are chosen can also say hallelujah because He is an omniscient God as it is written in the Old Testament:

> 2 Chronicles 16:9 (KJV): *"For the eyes of the Lord run to and fro throughout the whole earth, to shew himself strong in the*

C.H.O.S.E.N.

behalf of them whose heart is perfect toward him."

Proverbs 15:3 (NIV): *"The eyes of the Lord are everywhere, keeping watch on the wicked and the good."*

Hallelujah is the highest form of exhortation or praise. It is a very common expression and should be used as the chosen communication and the chosen daily conversation. It is a good pattern to practice for living life and living it more abundantly. We don't say hallelujah with our mouths without saying hallelujah with our lives. Our hallelujah talk should match our hallelujah walk. When our walk and talk come together, we can raise a hallelujah to our God.

The song, "Raise a Hallelujah," written by Jonathan David Helser, Melissa Helser, and Molly Skaggs and published by Bethel Music[6], raises a hallelujah praise to Jesus. Here is an excerpt from the song…try singing it in your spirit:

> I raise a hallelujah, in the presence of my enemies
> I raise a hallelujah, louder than the unbelief
> I raise a hallelujah, my weapon is a melody
> I raise a hallelujah, Heaven comes to fight for me

Here are the reasons I've been chosen to raise my hallelujahs. I've got some stories to tell. I need to testify.

1. In 1983, I was informed that due to female issues I would never be able to have any children. But God's report was different. When the doctors said no, my God said yes. Without medical help, but

Angie M. R. Gatlin

with God's miracle-working power, I have three anointed children. On March 3rd, 1988, I gave birth to a son and named him Angelo Geovonte DeShawn. On September 13th, 1990, I gave birth to another son and named him De'Angelo Cortez, and on September 9th, 1998, I gave birth to a daughter and named her Angel Maresha LeShai. Notice Angelo is Italian/Greek, and it means "messenger sent from God." DeAngelo is Italian, and it means "from the angel." Angel is Greek, and it means "messenger of God."

2. In 2002 and 2010, I experienced lumps on my breast and was sent to the Breast Cancer Center. Both times, there were no treatments and the lumps disappeared. I have been chosen to say hallelujah!

3. I have been chosen to say hallelujah for my education. I graduated from high school in 1977 from the 11th grade. God allowed me to skip the 12th grade, and I graduated from Henderson State University on May 15th, 1981 with a Bachelor of Science in Social Work. I was 16 when I went to college, and I graduated when I was 20. And I raise a hallelujah that I was able to go to college debt-free.

4. I raise a hallelujah that my household got the coronavirus in July 2020, but our great God healed us all. Millions didn't make it and are still dealing with this virus, and as I write this book, there have been 833,029 who have died due to the virus with my brother Michael being in that number ...but God!

C.H.O.S.E.N.

5. I raise a hallelujah that God chose me to carry His gospel. My journey began in 1995. I accepted my calling to preach in 2001 at Setting the Captivity Free Ministry in Stuttgart, Arkansas. I was ordained on December 20th, 2009, by my husband, Pastor Charles Gatlin. I wouldn't take anything for my journey. To God be the glory for the things He has done and is doing in my life.

You ought to take a little time and say hallelujah to Jesus. You got a right and reasons to say it!

- Hallelujah! Today, I get to breathe.
- Hallelujah! Your mercies are new every morning.
- Hallelujah! For You are my present help.
- Hallelujah! You are my joy in sorrow and my hope for tomorrow.
- Hallelujah! You are my calm in the midst of my storms.
- Hallelujah! You are a bridge over my troubled waters.
- Hallelujah! You are my strength like no other.
- Hallelujah! You are my doctor in a sick room and my lawyer in the courtroom.
- Hallelujah! You are my water in dry places.
- Hallelujah! You are my bread in a starving land.
- Hallelujah! You are a burden bearer and a heavy load sharer.
- Hallelujah! You give me beauty for my ashes.

- Hallelujah! You give me the oil of joy for my mourning.
- Hallelujah! You give me a garment of praise for my heaviness.
- Hallelujah! You are my way out, my way over, my way through, my way under, and my way out of no way.

The psalmist gives us reasons to say hallelujah:

> Psalm 9:1 (KJV): *"I will praise thee, O Lord, with my whole heart; I will shew forth all thy marvelous works."*
>
> Psalm 136:1 (NASB): *"Give thanks to the Lord for he is good; for his loving kindness is everlasting."*
>
> Psalm 100:4 (NIV): *"Enter his gates with thanksgiving and his courts with praise. Give thanks to Him, bless his name."*
>
> Psalm 113:3 (KJV): *"From the rising of the sun unto the going down of the same the Lord's name is to be praised."*
>
> Psalm 56:12 (NIV): *"I am under vows to you, my God; I will present my thank offerings to you."*
>
> Psalm 34: 1-8 (KJV): *"I will bless the Lord at all times: his praise shall continually be in my mouth. My soul shall make her boast in the Lord: the humble shall hear thereof, and be glad. O magnify the Lord with me,*

C.H.O.S.E.N.

and let us exalt his name together. I sought the Lord, and he heard me, and delivered me from all my fears. They looked unto him, and were lightened: and their faces were not ashamed. This poor man [girl] cried, and the Lord heard him [her], saved him [her] out of all his her] troubles. The angel of the Lord encampeth round about them that fear him, and delivereth them. O taste and see that the Lord is good: blessed is the man that trusteth in him."

All of these verses are just the tip of the iceberg; there are so many bible scriptures that tell us to praise the Lord and to shout hallelujah.

My good friend and radio host at KABF 88.3 (where he allows me to co-host with him), Pastor Maurice Tatum often says, "There are two times to praise God, when you feel like it and when you don't feel like it." Not only does Pastor Tatum say this, but he has no problem letting his feet get light, his hands lift high, and his tongue get loose. And if you know him, he will let a praise break through.

No matter what's going on or what condition you find *yourself in, no matter whether your money is funny and* your change is strange, no matter if you are having a good day or a bad day, you are still commanded to praise God. We, the chosen, are required to bless His holy name at all times. We have to look past circumstances and/or situations and cling to the Cross.

Because we are chosen to say hallelujah, we must count it as all joy when we fall into many temptations (James 1:2 KJV).

Angie M. R. Gatlin

We stand on the promise of 2 Peter 2:9 (KJV): *"The Lord knoweth how to deliver the godly out of temptations, and to reserve the unjust unto the Day of Judgment to be punished."*

When you are chosen to say hallelujah, you take your eyes off the problem and put them on the problem solver.

When you are chosen to say hallelujah, you take your eyes off your burdens and put them on the burden bearer.

When you are chosen to say hallelujah, you take your eyes off your troubles and put them on the troubleshooter.

When we are chosen to say hallelujah and give praise to God, we turn our hearts from ourselves toward the One we were made (chosen) to adore. So, as those who are chosen to say hallelujah, we shall raise our voices as creatures here below and mingle with the saints that have gone before us and with the heavenly host to give praise to the Author and Finisher of our faith, to the One who gives us a living hope, even on dark days.

It is a commandment and a duty that belong to each of us individually and collectively.

The psalmist said it best in Psalm 150:1-6 (KJV):

> *"Praise ye the Lord. Praise God in his sanctuary: praise him in the firmament of his power. Praise him for his mighty acts: praise him according to his excellent greatness. Praise him with the sound of the*

C.H.O.S.E.N.

trumpet: praise him with the psaltery and harp. Praise him with the timbrel and dance: praise him with stringed instruments and organs. Praise him upon the loud cymbals: praise him upon the high-sounding cymbals. Let everything that hath breath praise the Lord. Praise ye the Lord."

I am chosen to say HALLELUJAH!

Angie M. R. Gatlin

C.H.O.S.E.N.

Chapter 3

CHOSEN TO OVERCOME

1 Corinthians 15:57 (NIV): *"But thanks be to God! He gives us the victory through our Lord Jesus Christ."*

1 John 5:4 (NIV): *"For everyone born of God overcomes the world. This is the victory that has overcome the world, even our faith."*

Revelation 3:5 (KJV): *"He that overcometh, the same shall be clothed in white raiment; and I will not blot out his name out of the book of life, but I will confess his name before my Father, and before his angels."*

Revelation 2:11b (KJV): *"He that overcometh shall not be hurt of the second death."*

My Affirmation

I (YOUR NAME) have been chosen to Overcome.

What Exactly Does It Mean To Be Chosen To Overcome?

The word for *overcome* in the Greek language, according to Strong's Concordance is *nikao*, and it means victory, to conquer, to carry off the victory, or come off victorious. We must realize the world is a battle ground not a playground, a battleship, not a cruise ship. The Greek word *work nikao* is where we get the word *nike*, which means to be victorious in our struggles because we are chosen.

The Bible records in John 16:33 (NIV): *"I have told you these things, so that in me you may have peace. In this world you will have trouble. But take heart! I have overcome the world."*

Clarke's Commentary on the Bible[7] explains it like this: "That in me ye might have peace – I give you this warning as another proof that I know all things, and to the end that ye may look to me alone for peace and happiness."

When we are chosen to overcome, we remember that God will keep us in perfect peace when our minds stay on Him because we trust in Him (Isaiah 26:3 NKJV). There's an old saying that I heard as a child...Know God, Know Peace, No God, No Peace.

When the chosen acknowledge God, we have peace. When we shed darkness and sin and allow God's healing love to come in, there is a peace that no power can overcome:

> 1 Samuel 25:6 (ESV): *"Peace be to you, and peace be to your house, and peace be to all that you have."*
>
> Philippians 4:7 (ESV): *"And the peace that surpasses all understanding will guard your hearts and minds in Christ Jesus."*

What then is the peace of God?

Clark's Commentary on the Bible[7] explains it this way: "The peace of God is ever to be understood as including all possible blessedness – light, strength, comfort, support, a sense of divine favor, unction of the Holy Spirit, the purification of heart and the power to overcome anything.

Jesus gave those who were chosen to overcome a guarantee for the future in John 16:33 (KJV): *"...In the world, ye shall have tribulation..."* For the chosen, this

C.H.O.S.E.N.

guarantee implies three things: You are either in a battle, headed into a battle, or just coming out of a battle.

No matter where we are in the battle, we have no reason to fret or worry because 1 Samuel 17:47b (NIV) assures us that we are overcomers because the battle is the Lord's.

The beloved disciple closes John 16:33 by saying, *"...but be of good cheer."* We may ask, "Why should we be of good cheer? Here is the answer - Jesus has overcome the world.

Come what may we will overcome because we will have life more abundantly (John 10:10 NKJV). Come what may we will overcome because we will count it all joy. Count is a verb that means to determine the total number or the action or process of counting. It is also a financial term that means "to evaluate."

Counting it all joy, for the overcomers, will help us to evaluate the way we look at trials. James 1:2 calls for overcomers to develop a new attitude and not get caught off guard when sudden trials come our way, but we can stand firm and declare God is our way maker, miracle worker, promise keeper and the light in the darkness.

We hold on to that joy while we go through the process of becoming overcomers as Peter explains in 1 Peter 1:6-7 (NIV): *"In all this you greatly rejoice, though now for a little while you may have had to suffer grief in all kinds of trial. These have come so that the proven genuineness of your faith – of greater worth than gold, which perishes even though refined by fire – may result in praises, glory and honor when Jesus is revealed."*

We are overcomers because of Christ and because we belong to Christ.

Clarke's Commentary of the Bible[7] says, "My [our] apparent weakness shall be victory; my ignominy shall be my glory; and the victory which the world, the devil, and my adversaries in general, shall appear to gain over me, shall be their own lasting defeat, and my eternal triumph - Fear not!

These two words, "Fear not," are in the Bible 365 times to remind the overcomer that we can depend on the sovereign goodness of God, not by what might be or what we imagine could be. "Fear not" is the most repeated command in the Bible. In fact, it's been said that these 365 "Fear not's" in the bible give us one "Fear not" for every day of the year!

I love how the psalmist explains it in Psalm 56:3-4 (NIV): *"When I am afraid, I will trust you. In God, whose word I praise, In God I trust; I will not be afraid. What can mortal man do to me?"*

When you are chosen to overcome, it doesn't mean you will breeze through life without any opposition or obstacles in your way. But an overcomer is one who realizes each day will present another problem, another barrier, another obstacle that stands in the way or another opponent who criticizes you. Being an overcomer has nothing to do with the circumstances around you, but it has everything to do with the commitment inside you, because greater is he who is in you that he who is in the world (1John 4:4b KJV).

C.H.O.S.E.N.

Because we are overcomers, we accept the promise of God's word that no matter how great the problem, we can overcome:

> 1 John 4:4a (KJV): *"Ye are of God, little children, and have overcome them:"*
>
> 1 John 4:4a (NLT): *"But you belong to God, my dear children. You have already won a victory over those people,"*
>
> 1 John 5:4-5 (ESV): *"For everyone who has been born of God overcomes the world. And this is the victory that has overcome the world – our faith. Who is it that overcomes the world, except the one who believes that Jesus is the Son of God?"*

Overcomers are followers of Christ and those who endure when times get difficult. Now this doesn't mean it will be easy, but it will be worth it.

Overcomers completely depend on God for direction, purpose, fulfillment and strength. They trust in the Lord with all their hearts and lean not to their own understanding as they acknowledge Him in all their ways and allow Him to direct their paths (Proverbs 3:5-6 KJV).

Here's how He directs an overcomer's life:

- The Lord is BEFORE us – John 10:4 (ESV): *"When he has brought out all his own, he goes before them, and the sheep follow him, for they know his voice."*

- The Lord is BEHIND us – Psalm 139:15 (KJV): *"Thou has beset me behind and before, and laid thine hand upon me."*

- The Lord is ABOVE us – Ephesians 4:6 (KJV): *"One God and Father of all, who is above all, and through all, and in you all.*

- The Lord is AROUND us – Psalm 125:2 (KJV): *"As the mountains are round about Jerusalem, so the Lord is round about his people henceforth even forever."*

- The Lord is WITH us – Isaiah 41:10 (KJV): *"Fear thou not; for I am with thee: be not dismayed; for I am thy God: I will strengthen thee; yea, I will help thee; yea, I will uphold thee with the right hand of righteousness."*

- The LORD is in the MIDST of us – Zephaniah 3:17 (KJV): *"The Lord thy God in the midst of thee is mighty; he will save, he will rejoice over thee with joy; he will rest in his love, he will joy over thee with singing."*

When the chosen overcomers allow God to direct their steps and paths, then and only then, will the uncommon happen, the unusual occur, the unbelievable transpire, the unexplainable result, the unpredictable surface, and the unsurpassable emerge. That God of ours can turn your failures into success, your enemies into friends, your sorrows into joy, your duties into delights, your miseries into miracles, your deficiencies into sufficiency and your frustrations into faith.

C.H.O.S.E.N.

In 2 Corinthians 12:9 (MSG), Paul states, but he said to me, *"My grace is sufficient for you, for my power is made perfect in weakness."* Therefore, I will boast all the more gladly about my weaknesses, so that Christ's power may rest on me.

God's grace is for whosoever and under whatsoever circumstances the overcomer faces. God's grace for the chosen makes heavy burdens bearable, high mountains climbable, deep valleys crossable, painful sufferings endurable, big disappointments faceable, lonely nights livable, and daily pressures manageable.

God's grace goes a little further to reveal itself:

- To the hopeless by giving them hope.
- To the perplexed by giving them peace.
- To the sad by giving them joy.
- To the weak by giving them strength.
- To the helpless by giving them help.
- To the lonely by giving them comfort.
- To the weary by giving them inspiration.
- To the chosen by giving them free access.

There are no waiting lines, and nobody is turned away. There are no established hours of operation, but the overcomer is welcome morning, noon or night. We have 24/7 access. All the overcomer has to do is ask. It is God that does the supplying. The Bible plainly states in Matthew 7: 7-8 (KJV): *"Ask, and it shall be given you; seek, and ye shall find; knock, and it shall be opened unto you: For everyone that asketh receiveth; and he that seeketh findeth; and to him that knocketh it shall be opened."*

As overcomers, we don't need references; no resume is required. In Revelation 3:20 (KJV), it says, *"Behold, I stand at the door, and knock. If any man hears my voice, and opens the door, I will come into him, and will sup with him, and he with me."*

Take some time to meditate on the great promises and rewards that Apostle John left for those who overcome in the book of Revelation:

- Overcomers will eat from the Tree of Life (Revelation 2:7).
- Overcomers will not be harmed by the second death (Revelation 2:11).
- Overcomers will eat from hidden manna and be given a new name (Revelation 2:17).
- Overcomers will have authority over nations (Revelation 2:26).
- Overcomers will be clothed in white garments (Revelation 3:5).
- Overcomers will be made a permanent pillar in the house of God (Revelation 3:12).
- Overcomers will sit with Jesus on His throne (Revelation 3:21).

C.H.O.S.E.N.

- Overcomers defeat the enemy by the blood of the Lamb and by the word of their testimony, and they love not their lives unto death (Revelation 12:11).

I am chosen to OVERCOME!

_____
_____
_____
_____
_____
_____
_____
_____
_____
_____
_____
_____
_____
_____
_____

Angie M. R. Gatlin

C.H.O.S.E.N.

Chapter 4

CHOSEN TO SERVE

Joshua 24:15a (NIV): *"But if serving the Lord seems undesirable to you, then choose for yourselves this day whom you will serve."*

Galatians 5:13 (NIV): *"You, my brothers and sisters, were called to be free. But do not use your freedom to indulge the fresh; rather, serve one another humbly in love."*

1 Samuel 12:24 (NIV): *"But be sure to fear the Lord and serve him faithfully with all*

C.H.O.S.E.N.

your heart; consider what great things he has done for you."

John 12:26 (KJV): *"If any man serves me, let him follow me; and where I am, there shall also my servant be; if any man serves, me, him will my Father honour."*

Matthew 9:37 (KJV): *"Then saith he unto his disciples, the harvest truly is plenteous, but the labourers are few;"*

My Affirmation

I (YOUR NAME) Have Been Chosen to Serve.

WHAT EXACTLY DOES IT MEAN TO BE CHOSEN TO SERVE?

◆―――――――――――――――◆

The word *serve* in the Greek language is *diakoneo* according to the Strong Concordance. It means "to attend to anything, to minister a thing to one, or to be a servant.

I have been a manager for 35+years. Within those years, I have had the opportunity to meet and hire so many different types of people. During that time, I never hired anyone just to give them benefits. I hired them to do a job that would benefit the company. Once they were hired, they would receive benefits after their 90-day probation period.

Angie M. R. Gatlin

For those of us who are chosen to serve, there are many benefits. We are provided with salvation and eternal life, we have a relationship with the Father, we are adopted into the family of God, we are joint-heirs with Jesus, we have a home in Heaven, and we have the opportunity for an abundant life on earth. But God did not just save us to keep us from Hell. He did not just save us simply to give us a mansion in Heaven. Our ultimate purpose in this life is to bring honor and glory to our Heavenly Father. If that is true (and chosen saints, it is), then it is safe to say we were saved to serve.

We are called, commanded, commissioned, and chosen to share the Gospel for the remainder of our lives. And if you are like me, I've got more years behind me than I do in front of me (words often expressed by Charles Gatlin).

To be called requires us to quickly carry out the tasks assigned us by the one who sent us (John 9:4 NLT). To be commissioned means that our meat is to do the will of him that sent us and to finish his work (John 4:34 KJV). When we who are chosen to serve by sharing the Good News, we must be willing to do the work, do it with all our might and be on one accord while serving (Ecclesiastes 9:10 KJV).

Being in the food service business for years granted me the opportunity to motivate employees to work even when others were not willing to work. My department motto was "teamwork makes a dream work," because I believed the whole was greater than the sum of its parts. Teamwork meant that people would try to cooperate by using their individual skills to achieve the ultimate goal.

C.H.O.S.E.N.

It also involved knowing the three types of workers in business: those who made things happen, those who watched things happen, and those who had no notion of what was happening. While serving as a manager, I kept a poem at the clock in station as a tool to encourage my employees with positive emotions like pride, a sense of belonging, and the thrill of achievement. This poem gave them multiple reasons for doing what I needed them to do and ensure the completion of the job task, and I believe, beyond a shadow of a doubt, that the Bible was (and will always be) our manual for us to use to complete the work of ministry.

Here is the poem[8]:

> *This is a little story about four people named Everybody, Somebody, Anybody, and Nobody.*
>
> *There was an important job to be done and Everybody was sure that Somebody would do it.*
>
> *Anybody could have done it, but Nobody did it.*
>
> *Somebody got angry about that because it was Everybody's job.*
>
> *Everybody thought that Anybody could do it, but Nobody realized that Everybody wouldn't do it.*
>
> *It ended up that Everybody blamed Somebody when Nobody did what Anybody could have done.*

Angie M. R. Gatlin

-Author Unknown

The joy of working for the Lord is everybody is somebody, and there's no big I's or little u's. There's no me, myself and I. The apostle Paul explains it best in 1 Corinthians 12:12-27 (KJV):

> "For as the body is one, and hath many members, and all the members of that one body, being many, are one body: so also is Christ. For by one Spirit are we all baptized into one body, whether we be Jews or Gentiles, whether we be bond or free; and have been all made to drink into one Spirit. For the body is not one member, but many. If the foot shall say, because I am not the hand, I am not of the body; is it therefore not of the body? And if the ear shall say, because I am not the eye, I am not of the body; is it therefore not of the body? If the whole body were an eye, where were the hearing? If the whole were hearing, where were the smelling? But now hath God set the members every one of them in the body, as it hath pleased him. And if they were all one member, where were the body? But now are they many members, yet but one body. And the eye cannot say unto the hand, I have no need of thee: nor again the head to the feet, I have no need of you. Nay, much more those members of the body, which seem to be more feeble, are necessary: And those members of the body, which we think to be

less honourable, upon these we bestow more abundant honour; and our uncomely parts have more abundant comeliness. For our comely parts have no need: but God hath tempered the body together, having given more abundant honour to that part which lacked. That there should be no schism in the body; but that the members should have the same care one for another. And whether one member suffer, all the members suffer with it; or one member be honoured, all the members rejoice with it. Now ye are the body of Christ and individually members of it."

Being chosen to serve has to do with whose we are, whom we serve, and how much we give of ourselves in commitment, devotion, and service. Service carries a price tag for the chosen (Matthew 22:37 NIV; Matthew 6:24 KJV). My friend Kim Smith says, "What your heart possesses, your life expresses."

Service is often misunderstood. Many Christians regard it as something extra that they will give to the Lord only when they have spare time and effort for it. To them, it is optional. We must understand that service is not an option, but a requirement. It is a sin to short-change God, to give God our leftovers, and to offer God less than our best.

Kim also says, "We all have an amount of time destined by God." In that time, we choose what we do and what we want. We choose what we strive for and who our lives influence. We choose God or other things. God loves us always, regardless of what we choose.

But when our time is done, we get what we've chosen. What we have chosen, not what God chose for us. We can choose God or we can choose to be without Him. But it's for eternity. So, seek the Lord while He can be found.

Are we cheating God with our service? Are we aware of how much we owe God?
Are we aware that we owe a debt that we could not pay? But Jesus paid it all, and all to Him we owe.

The psalmist asked a question in Psalm 116:12 (BSB): *"How can I repay the Lord for all his goodness to me?"* The KJV translation puts it like this, "What shall I render unto the LORD for all his benefits toward me?" This is a universal question for those who are chosen to serve. It is a prerequisite of service and a necessary condition. I've discovered that if we be about God's business, He will be about our business.

So, my beloved, will you give your three T's – Your Time, Your Talent and Your Treasure? If your answer is yes, then answer these five questions:

1. How much is enough?
2. What proportion is proper?
3. What figure is fair?
4. How much time is tangible?
5. What sacrifice is sufficient?

It isn't enough to know what to do...we must do it! It is not about what we want to do, but that we must do it!

C.H.O.S.E.N.

Service should never feel like a chore as followers of Christ.

As it says in Psalm 100:2 (NASB), *"Serve the Lord with gladness; come before Him with joyful singing."* We must also do what Paul advised Timothy to do in 2 Timothy 1:6 (NKJV): *"Therefore, I remind you to stir up the gift of God with is in you. You do know what we are is God gift to us, but what we do with ourselves is our gift to God."*

The late self-help author Oliver Napoleon Hill said, "If you cannot do great things, do small things in a great way." He also said, "The man who does more than he is paid for will soon be paid for more than he does." And one of his famous quotes that has impacted my life is "Procrastination is the bad habit of putting off until the day after tomorrow what should have been done the day before yesterday."

Pastor Charles Gatlin often says, "Never pray: Lord, bless me. Instead, pray: Lord make me a blessing." He often reminds the members of Evangelistic Baptist Church that we are not saved by serving, but because we are saved, we serve.

When one is chosen to serve, he or she lives out the three R's of service:

1. Rearrange – Rearrange your schedule.
2. Render – Render some service.
3. Release – Release some silver.

My friend Ann Rice shared a principle with me that has impacted my life. It is called the Rebecca Principle. Mrs.

Angie M. R. Gatlin

Rice said, "It is doing more than what you are required to do and then some. Many others say it is to do all you can to do all you can. Never stick to the expected, go beyond."

This principle is derived from Genesis 24: 17-19 in which we get a description in great detail of how Rebekah comes to be the wife of Abraham's son Isaac:

> *And the servant ran to meet her, and said, let me, I pray thee, drink a little water of thy pitcher. And she said, Drink, my lord: and she hasted, and let down her pitcher upon her hand, and gave him drink. And when she had done giving him drink, she said, I will draw water for thy camels also, until they have done drinking.*

There are three important qualities of the Rebekah Principle:

1. *Abound in giving* – When Abraham's servant asked her for a drink of water, she happily gave it to him without question.

2. *Anticipate the needs of others* – After giving Abraham's servant a drink, she recognized that his camels needed water and immediately acted by giving them water as well.

3. *Serve without complaining* – Rebekah did these things without once complaining about it. She had a servant's heart.

C.H.O.S.E.N.

This ought to be our daily prayer – God, forgive me for applying minimal effort and expecting maximum return. Please provide opportunities for me to step beyond what is convenient and comfortable and meet the needs of someone else. Develop in me a servant's heart.

My testimony is whatsoever Angie's hand findeth to do, I will do it with all my might! (Romans 12:11 NLT; Colossians 3:23-24 NIV)

Paul reminds the chosen that regardless of our station in life, God is our ultimate judge and all of our service is really for HIM. We are not to merely "get by" with the bare minimum of what we are obligated to do. But we should make our work count! None of us should want to get to the end of our lives and say, "What was that all about?" We are only given so many minutes in the hour, so many hours in the day, so many days in the week, so many weeks in a month, so many months in a year, and so many years on the calendar.

I have started counting my years as months, my months as weeks, my weeks as days, my days as hours, my hours as minutes, and my minutes as seconds. My mother often said, "Time waits on no one." The Bible also says how important it is to have lived a life that shows someone serving the Lord in obedience:

> Hebrews 9:27 (KJV): *"And as it is appointed unto men once to die, but after this the judgment:"*

> Revelation 13:14 (KJV): *"And I heard a voice from heaven saying unto me, Write, Blessed are the dead which die in the Lord*

Angie M. R. Gatlin

form henceforth: yea, saith the Spirit, that they may rest from their labours; and their works do follow them."

We have established that God doesn't call or choose the qualified, but He will qualify the call. We have established that God doesn't call or choose us for our abilities, but our availabilities. Now let's establish what it means to be chosen to serve.

When we are chosen to serve, we know:

- The field is large. Matthew 13:38 (KJV): *"The field is the world."*

- The need is great. John 4:35 (NIV): *"I tell you, open your eyes and look at the fields! They are ripe for harvest."*

- The time is now. John 9:4 (KJV): *"I must work the works of him that sent me, while it its day: the night cometh, when no man can work."*

- The call is urgent. Matthew 20:6 (KJV): *"And about the eleventh hour he went out, and found others standing idle, and saith unto them, why stand ye here all the day idle?"*

- The partner is Almighty. 2 Corinthians 6:1 (NLT): *"As God's partners, we beg you not to accept this marvelous gift of God's kindness and then ignore it."*

- The means are provided. Philippians 4:19 (NLT): *"And this same God who takes care of*

C.H.O.S.E.N.

me will supply all your needs from his glorious riches, which have been given to us in Christ Jesus."

Ecclesiastes 3:1 (NIV) says, *"There is a time for everything and a season for every activity under the heavens."* I believe that it is high time for those who are chosen to gear up and take our right position in the Lord's army.

I am chosen to SERVE!

_____
_____
_____
_____
_____
_____
_____
_____
_____
_____
_____
_____
_____
_____
_____

Angie M. R. Gatlin

C.H.O.S.E.N.

Chapter 5

CHOSEN TO ENDURE

Matthew 24:13 (KJV): *"But he that shall endure unto the end, the same shall be saved."*

James 5:11 (KJV): *"Behold, we count them happy which endure."*

1 Corinthians 10:13 (ESV): *"No temptation has overtaken you that is not common to man. God is faithful, and he will not let you be tempted beyond your ability. But with the*

C.H.O.S.E.N.

temptation he will also provide the way of escape, that you may be able to endure it."

Philippians 4:13 (NKJV): *"I can do all things Christ who strengthens me."*

My Affirmation

I (YOUR NAME) have been chosen to Endure.

What Exactly Does It Mean To Be Chosen To Endure?

The word *endure* in the Greek language is *hypomeno* according to Strong Concordance. It means to persevere, absolutely and emphatically under misfortunes and trials to hold fast to one's faith in Christ.

When we are faced with the storms of life, we sometimes aren't sure that we will make it through. However, we may find that we bend and feel like we are not going to get through it. If we stand our ground and exhibit persistence and determination, we will make it through.

Watching a tree in a storm and seeing the wind bend the tree, you expect the tree to fall over. But when the roots of the tree are deep within the ground, the tree sways back and forth with the wind - no matter how strong the wind is.

Angie M. R. Gatlin

Our lives are like that. Each storm makes us stronger to face the next one. Our attitude and beliefs can keep us grounded and help us as we face life's challenges. I encourage you to be like a tree when faced with issues in life. We can endure much more than we may imagine. We just have to stay grounded and stay true to our roots. And, it goes without saying stay true to yourself and your values! Hang in there, always remembering the storms of life do pass, the winds will die down, and the sunshine and blue skies do appear again. After all, we serve a God who can say, "Peace be still," and even the winds and the waves will obey Him.

The Bible records in Matthew 24:13 (KJV): *"But he that shall endure unto the end, the same shall be saved."* This verse is part of the Jesus Olivet Discourse, an explanation to the disciples about things to come.

Endure means to "abide under," "to bear up courageously," or "to tarry or wait." 1 Thessalonians 1:3 (NIV) gives us another perspective on what it means to endure: *"We remember before our God and Father your work produced by faith, your labor prompted by love and your endurance inspired by hope in our Lord Jesus Christ."*

The picture of endurance is the ability to hang on when it would have been easier to let go. Many people are blessed with different attributes, but to endure is at the top of the list for success in any endeavor.

When you are chosen to endure, it means you will not give up or let go. When you are chosen to endure, you have the power to go on in spite of difficulties.

C.H.O.S.E.N.

Familiar conversations or words or expressions used in ordinary language by common people to explain *endure* are "keep on keeping on," "hang in there," "put up with it," "stick-to-itiveness," and "Don't quit." Its synonyms are determination, perseverance, tenacity, plodding, stamina, and backbone.

> Isaiah 43: 1-3 (NKJV) But now, thus says the LORD, who created you, O Jacob, And He who formed you, O Israel: "Fear not, for I have redeemed you: I have called you by your name: You are Mine.

When you pass through the waters, I will be with you. When you walk through the fire, you shall not be burned, Nor shall the flame scorch you. For I am the LORD your God. The Holy One of Israel, your Savior;

Being chosen to endure means hold on for dear life! Franklin D. Roosevelt, the 32nd President of the United States said, "When you reach the end of your rope, tie a knot in it and hang on." Angie Gatlin says it this way, "When you get to the end of the rope, tie a knot in it and hang on because help is on the way."

The Bible describes holding on during adversity like this:

> Psalm 46:1 (NIV): *"God is our refuge and strength an ever-present help in trouble."*
>
> Psalm 34:17 (NIV): *"When the righteous cry for help, the Lord hears, and rescues them from all their troubles."*

Angie M. R. Gatlin

Proverb 18:10 (KJV): *"The name of the LORD is a strong tower: the righteous run to it and are safe."*

No one enjoys suffering, but suffering is a necessary normal part of the Christian life. As a matter of fact, the Scripture says we are to expect hardships and suffering to increase (2 Timothy 2:3-4 KJV).

I had the opportunity to be the child of a good soldier. His name is James Henry Roberts, and he was a chosen soldier, my father, my friend, my go to for anything person.

On Memorial Day in 2014, we received the tear-jerking news that he had stage 4 colon cancer. We had to make the decision to allow it to run its course or to do chemo. As my nine siblings and I met with Mom and Dad to make the dreadful decision, he only had one request, "Don't let me suffer." Those four words will remain in my ears for the rest of my life.

My father endured three weeks of chemo, and the Master took him home on December 10th, 2014 @ 9:30 p.m. His body is not here, but his love is still here with me, and I feel his very presence from time to time. But just to know he is no longer suffering and that he is resting in the bosom of the Master is good enough for me.

I am the child of another good solider, her name is Geneva Roberts, my mother, my friend, my go to for anything and the meekest person I know.

C.H.O.S.E.N.

My mother was diagnosed with Alzheimer about 10 years ago and she has fought it like a good solider, she is enduring as this progressive disease has destroys her memory and all of her mental functions. She is bedridden, has to be bath and feed. She doesn't know I am there to help her, but the main thing is I know that I am there for her. I will walk this chapter of her life journey as she endures until the Master comes for her or me.

Life can certainly get rough and tough, crude and unjust. But it is in those trying moments that we find strength in God that we didn't realize we had, and we become more that we ever were before (1 Cor. 10:13 KJV; 2 Tim. 2:12 NAS; 1 Peter 4:12 KJV).

Suffering will indeed come, but God can give us grace and power to overcome every trial and to fulfill our purpose and mission in His kingdom.

When it comes to the subject of being chosen to endure, we all should feel the same as we feel about going to heaven: we're all for it, but we'd rather not go through what we have to go through to get there!

It's still true; He will pull you through if you can stand the pull (Exodus 15:2 NLT).

> *The Lord is my strength and my song; he has given me victory. This is my God, and I will praise him—my father's God, and I will exalt him!*

It's still true; if He brings you to it, He will bring you through it (Deuteronomy 3:6 ESV).

Angie M. R. Gatlin

And we devoted them to destruction, as we did to Sihon the king of Heshbon, devoting to destruction every city, men, women, and children.

When we are chosen to endure, God will give us seven elements to direct us:

1. <u>Courage</u> to fight the battle. Joshua 1:9 (NIV): *"Have I not commanded you? Be strong and courageous. Do not be afraid, do not be discouraged, for the Lord your God will be with you wherever you go."*

2. <u>Strength</u> to run the race. Psalm 27:1 (KJV): *"The Lord is my light and my salvation; whom shall I fear? The Lord is the strength of my life: of whom shall I be afraid?"*

3. <u>Peace</u> in the midst of the storm. Isaiah 26:3 (CSB): *"You will keep the mind that is dependent on you in perfect peace, for it is trusting in you."*

4. <u>Boldness</u> to press toward the mark. Philippians 3:13-14 (KJV): *"Brethren, I count not myself to have apprehended: but this one thing I do, forgetting those things which are behind, and reaching forth unto those things which are before. I press toward the mark for the prize of the high calling of God in Christ Jesus."*

5. <u>Ability</u> to stand the pressure. (KJV): *"Wherefore take unto you the whole armor of God that ye may be able to withstand in the evil day, and having done all, to stand. Stand therefore, having your*

C.H.O.S.E.N.

loins girt about with truth, and having on the breastplate of righteousness."

6. <u>Determination</u> to persevere. James 1:12 (KJV): *"Blessed is the man who perseveres under trial; for once he has been approved, he will receive the crown of life which the lord has promised to those who love HIM."*

7. <u>Assurance</u> of a reward. Revelation 2:10d (ESV): *"Be faithful unto death, and I will give you the crown of life."*

When you are chosen to endure, there will be some "BUT GOD."

- The challenges may be great, BUT GOD is greater.
- The problems may be big, BUT GOD is bigger.
- The pressures may be tremendous, BUT GOD is sufficient.
- The opposition may be strong, BUT GOD is stronger.
- The obstacles are many, BUT GOD is still able.
- The burdens are heavy, BUT GOD is capable.

The apostle Paul puts it this way in 2 Corinthians 4: 8 -9 (KJV):

"We are troubled on every side, yet not distressed; we are perplexed, but not in despair; Persecuted, but not forsaken, cast down, but not destroyed;"

Paul was simply teaching us that what we suffer now can't be compared to the glory of heaven that awaits us! (Getting to Heaven is our #1 priority). In 2 Corinthians 4:16-17 (NET), he encourages us with these words:

> *"Therefore we do not despair, but even if our physical body is wearing away, our inner person is being renewed day by day. For our momentary, light suffering is producing for us an eternal weight of glory far beyond all comparison."*

Nothing is impossible to the man who doesn't have to do it by himself (Philippians 4:13).

I am chosen to ENDURE!

C.H.O.S.E.N.

Angie M. R. Gatlin

Chapter 6

CHOSEN TO NEVER QUIT

Galatians 6:9 (NIV): *"Let us not become weary in doing good, for at the proper time we will reap a harvest if we do not give up."*

Ecclesiastes 9:11b (KJV): *"That the race is not to the swift, nor the battle to the strong."*

1 Corinthians 15:58 (KJV): *"Therefore, my beloved brethren, be ye steadfast, unmovable, always abounding in the work of the*

Angie M. R. Gatlin

LORD, forasmuch as ye know that your labour is not in vain in the LORD."

2 Cor. 4:17-18 (NIV): *"For our light and momentary troubles are achieving for us an eternal glory that far outweighs them all. So we fix our eyes not on what is seen, but on what is unseen, since what is seen is temporary, but what is unseen is eternal."*

My Affirmation

I (YOUR NAME) have been chosen to NEVER QUIT!

What Exactly Does It Mean To Be Chosen To Never Quit?

◆━━━━━━━━━━━━━━━━━━━━◆

The word *quit* in the Greek language is *enkataleipo*, according to Strong Concordance.
When *quit* is used as a verb, it means:

- to desert, abandon, give up, forsake, drop out
- to put an end to a state or an activity
- give up or retire from a position
- go away or leave
- turn away from; give up
- give up in the face of defeat of lacking hope; admit defeat

Feeling exhausted, not sure whether to sit, stand, walk or run. When your schedule is crammed and you have a

C.H.O.S.E.N.

list of never-ending responsibilities always attempting to multitask it all in an effort to be more efficient, yet in the process ending up emotionally and physically fatigued.

Does this sound familiar to you?

I am just like you. We all have days where we're running on empty, and no matter how hard we work, the list of things to do just seems to get longer and longer.

When I feel the spirit of quitting sneaking up on me, I remember the 5 Statement Pledge of Faith[9] written by the American evangelist, author and Bible teacher, Beth Moore. She identifies what each finger represents in her Bible study on believing God:

- *Thumb* – God is who He says He is.
- *Index finger* – God can do what He says He can do.
- *Middle finger* – I am who God says I am.
- *Ring finger* – I can do all things through Christ.
- *Pinkie finger* – His word is alive and active in me.

Remember when God places a promise in your heart, you have to come to the place where you believe it's going to happen so strongly that you refuse to quit. You believe so strongly that nothing can talk you out of it or make you doubt it. It may seem impossible, and all the circumstances may tell you to quit because it's not going to happen; however, deep within, you have this burning confidence and this knowing that God is still on the throne.

Angie M. R. Gatlin

He has already made a way, and in God's time, what He promised will come to pass. You must have this "I can't quit" mindset, because your faith in God is unshakeable, unbreakable, and undeniable. I will believe the invisible, I will see the impossible, and I will receive the incredible.

You've got to know that God is fighting all of your battles, arranging things in your favor, manipulating the situation, and making a way when you don't see a way. When you are chosen to Never Quit instead of being discouraged, distracted or disgruntled, you get up in the morning thanking God that the answer is on the way.
Isaiah 43:19 (NIV) See, I am doing a new thing! Now it springs up; do you not perceive it? I am making away in the wilderness and streams in the wasteland.

When you are chosen to Never Quit, instead of talking about how big the problem is, you go through the day decreeing and declaring how big your God is. In Psalm 147:5 (ESV), the psalmist proclaims, *"Great is our Lord, and abundant in power; his understanding is beyond measure."*

A.W. Tozer, the American Christian pastor, author, magazine editor and spiritual mentor says, "Because God knows all things perfectly, he knows nothing better than any other thing, but all things equally well. He never discovers anything, he is never surprised, never amazed."[10]

When you are chosen to Never Quit, instead of murmuring and complaining, you look around, think things over, and thank God that it is working on your behalf with a purpose: And we know that all things work together for the good to them who love God and are the call according to his purpose (Roman 8:28 KJV).

C.H.O.S.E.N.

When you are chosen to Never Quit, your mind is set in one direction: victory, favor, healing, and restoration that births dedication. It may be taking a long time, but God didn't bring you this far to leave you. You've seen Him do it and you have watched Him do it, time after time, over and over, again and again. And you know He will do it again in the future.

It's simple… you can't quit! You've got to trust His timing, which is perfect.

Take notes on what King Solomon left on record in Ecclesiastes 3:1-8 (KJV):

> *To everything there is a season, and a time to every purpose under the heaven:*
>
> *A time to be born, and a time to die; a time to plant, and a time to pluck up that which is planted;*
>
> *A time to kill, and a time to heal; a time to break down, and a time to build up;*
>
> *A time to weep, and a time to laugh; a time to mourn, and a time to dance;*
>
> *A time to cast away stones, and a time to gather stones together; a time to embrace, and a time to refrain from embracing;*
>
> *A time to get, and a time to lose; a time to keep, and a time to cast away;*

Angie M. R. Gatlin

A time to rend, and a time to sew; a time to keep silence, and a time to speak;

A time to love, and a time to hate; a time of war, and a time of peace.

Jesus said in Luke 9:62 (KJV): *"No one that puts his hand to the plow and looks back is fit for service in the kingdom of God."* Those are strong words uttered from the Lord of the harvest. Christ phrased it that way because He knew that the Father would only reward those who endured.

I like the quote that says, "Winners never quit, and quitters never win." Amen! The same holds true in the Kingdom of God. Salvation belongs to those that "endure to the end" (Revelation 3). That's because the Christian race is not a 100-meter dash; it's a marathon! Winning a marathon requires endurance and running the race with patience. And for Christians, believing, trusting, hoping, persevering, and obeying God enable them to claim the victor's crown.

In the book of Revelation, Christ addressed the seven churches of Asia Minor. Each church received a similar exhortation from the Lord. To paraphrase Christ's words, He told them to "never give up."

- To the Church at Ephesus, He said: *"You have persevered and have endured hardships for my name, and have not grown weary. (2:3) . . . To him who overcomes, I will give the right to eat from the tree of life, which is in the paradise of God (2:7)."*

C.H.O.S.E.N.

- To the Church at Smyrna, He said: *"Be faithful, even to the point of death, and I will give you the crown of life* (2:10)."

- To the Church at Pergamum, He said: *"To him who overcomes, I will give some of the hidden manna* (2:17)."

- To the Church at Thyatira, He said: *"To him who overcomes and does my will to the end, I will give authority over the nations* (2:26)."

- To the Church at Sardis, He said: *"He who overcomes will, like them, be dressed in white. I will never blot out his name from the book of life but will acknowledge his name before my Father and his angels* (3:5)."

- *To the Church at Philadelphia,* He said: "Him who overcomes I will make a pillar in the temple of my God" (3:12).

- *To the Church at Laodicea*, He said: "To him who overcomes, I will give the right to sit with me on my throne, just as I overcame and sat down with my Father on his throne" (3:21).

Jesus promised His reward to those that remained faithful to the end! He promised the crown of life to those that finished the race!

We've all been there. We've all wanted to quit at some point in our lives. What I want you to understand first is that this is completely normal. Feeling like quitting is built into us. The moment when things get difficult and we are forced to change the status quo, our reflexes kick in to resist that change. There is a reason why many of us can't get up in the morning and go to the gym even though we know that it's good for us. Our brains are still wired for survival. This means that if we start on a difficult path, our brains will tell us to quit.

All of us, however, have a different quitting point. Over the years, you are likely to know your quitting point. Do you feel like quitting right after you start? Or just before you are about to reach your goal? Or when things start becoming unconventional and you are worried about what others will think about you?

What is your pattern when you decide to quit?

Or are you one of those people who just do not quit? Even if it means giving up everything.

The Bible says in Philippians 3:14 (MSG): *"...I've got my eye on the goal, where God is beckoning us onward...I'm off and running, and I'm not turning back!"*

- Don't Quit until God has wiped all the tears from your eyes, and there is no more death, neither sorrow, nor crying, neither shall there be any more pain (Revelation 21:4)

- Don't Quit until God renew your strength and restores your weary soul.
    - Isaiah 40:30 (KJV): *"Even youths shall faint and be weary."*

C.H.O.S.E.N.

- Hebrew 12:3 (ESV): *"Consider him who endured from sinners such hostility against himself, so that you may not grow weary or fainthearted."*

- Psalm 119:28 (NIV): *"My soul is weary with sorrow; strengthen me according to your word."*

- Jeremiah 31:25 (ESV): *"For I will satisfy the weary soul, and every languishing soul I will replenish."*

- Don't Quit until the last trump of God sounds.

- Don't Quit until your feet leave earth soils.

- Don't Quit until your body change.
- Don't Quit until corruption puts on incorruption and mortality puts on immortality (1 Corinthians 15:58)

- Don't Quit until we see Him….

    - High and lifted up (Isaiah 57:15).

    - As King of kings and Lord of lords (1 Timothy 6:15).

    - As the Prince of Peace (Isaiah 9:6).

    - As the Son of God (Luke 1:35).

- As the Firstborn from the Death (Revelation 1:5).
- As Alpha and Omega, the beginning and the end (Revelation 21:6).

- As the Author and Finisher of our Faith (Hebrews 12:2).

- As the First and the Last (Revelation 22:13).

- As the Lord, which is and which was, and which is to come, the Almighty (Revelation 1:8).

- <u>Don't Quit</u> until we see Him as John saw Him in Revelation 1:14-15 (NKJV): *"His head and his hairs were white like wool, as white as snow; and his eyes as a flame of fire; and his feet like unto fine brass, as if they burned in a furnace; and his voice as the sound of many waters."*

- <u>Don't Quit</u> until you hear the Master say, "Come up a little higher…..

    - Then the next step we will take will be on the streets of gold (Revelation 21:21).

    - Then the next breath we take will be the celestial atmosphere (Revelation 21: 1-5).

    - Then the next sight we will see will be the Resurrected Lamb sitteth on the right hand of the father (Mark 16:19).

C.H.O.S.E.N.

- Then the next meal we eat, will be at the Marriage Supper of the Lamb (Revelation 19:6-9).

- Then the next garment we wear, will be the white robe of righteousness (Revelation 6:11).

- Then the next gift we will receive will be the crown of life (James 1:12).

I am chosen to NEVER QUIT!

Angie M. R. Gatlin

C.H.O.S.E.N.

Conclusion

CROSSING THE FINISH LINE

Ecclesiastes 12:13-14 (KJV): *"Let's hear the conclusion of the whole matter: Fear God and keep his commandments: for this is the whole duty of man. For God shall bring every work into judgment with every secret thing, whether it be good, or whether it be evil."*

Hebrew 12:1-2 (KJV): *"Wherefore seeing we also are compassed about with so great a cloud of witnesses, let us lay aside every weight, and sin which doth so easily beset us, and let us run with patience the race that is set before us."*

John 14:1-6 (KJV): *"Let not your heart be troubled: ye believe, in God, believe also in me. In my Father's house are many mansions: if it were not so, I would have told you. I go to prepare a place for you. And if I go and prepare a place for you, I will come again, and receive you unto*

C.H.O.S.E.N.

myself; that where I am, there ye may be also. And whither I go ye know, and the way ye know. Thomas saith unto him, Lord, we know not whither thou goest; and how can we know the way. Jesus saith unto him, I am the way, the truth, and the life: no man cometh unto the Father, but by me."

Notice 3 statements for he Chosen

- Jesus said I am the way, when you are chosen without him there can be no going
- Jesus said I am the truth, when you are chosen, without him there can be no knowing
- Jesus said I am the life, when you are chosen, without him there can be no living

This poem is a great summary life's journey.

Life is but a stopping place,
A pause in what's to be,
A resting place along the road
To sweet eternity
We all have different journeys,
Different paths along the way,
We all are meant to learn some things
But never meant to stay....
Our destination is a place
Far greater that we know
For some, the journey's quicker,
For some, the journey's slow
And when the journey finally ends,
We'll claim a great reward
And find an everlasting place
Together with the LORD.
Author Unknown

Angie M. R. Gatlin

It is said that when one of his church members was dying, John Watson the Scottish, a preacher of Edinburgh, would kneel down and whisper in the person's ear, "In my Father's house are many rooms." Then, with a contented sign, the person would "slip away" entirely unafraid.

All of us are going to cross the finish line. We have no control of that. What we can control is HOW we will cross it. It states in Hebrew 9:27 (KJV), *"And as it is appointed unto men once to die, but after this the judgment,"* while 1 Corinthians (NKJV) describes what the race requires, *"Do you know that those who run in a race all run, but one receives the prize? Run in such a way that you may obtain it."*

After all, finishing the race is kind of the whole point.

When good runners are going to cross the finish line, they cross it with their arms pumping, their legs kicking, and their minds focused on finishing. I compare this illustration to a believer who is called home while still faithfully serving Christ and knowing that the prize we are running for is eternal life with Christ. It is being called home and being told, *"Well done good and faithful servant…enter into the joy of the LORD"* (Matthew 25:21 ESV). That is why we run to cross the finishing line.

Every life journey is paved with paths to travel, rivers to cross, mountains to climb, valleys to conquer, detours to distract us, and stops and speed bumps to overcome.

We don't always understand life's zigs and zags, twist and turns, ups and downs, or ins and outs, but we yield to the direction of the Lord to the path "we believe our Father has already chosen but not yet revealed to us"

C.H.O.S.E.N.

(quote from my friend, Kim Smith), and we lean on the promises of our God.

> Romans 4:21 (KJV): *"For all the promises of God in him are yea, and in him Amen, unto the glory of God by us."*

We lean on the love of our God that never changes.

> Jeremiah 31:3 (KJV): *"The LORD has appeared of old unto me, saying, yea, I have loved you with an everlasting love: therefore, with lovingkindness have I drawn you."*

We lean on the peace of our God.

> Isaiah 26:3 (KJV): *"Thou wilt keep him in perfect peace, whose mind is stayed on thee, because he trusteth in thee."*

> Philippians 4:6-8 (KJV): *"Be careful for nothing; but in everything by prayer and supplication with thanksgiving let your requests be made known unto God. And the peace of God which passeth all understanding, shall keep your hearts and minds through Christ Jesus. Finally brethren, whatsoever things are true, whatsoever things are honest, whatsoever things are just, whatsoever things are pure, whatsoever things are lovely, whatsoever things are of good report; if there be any virtue, and if there be any praise, think on these things."*

Angie M. R. Gatlin

There's a song called "Almost Home" recorded by Mercy Me, an American contemporary Christian music band founded in Edmond, Oklahoma. "Almost Home" is a kind of a rallying cry to just remind us to keep running the race…to keep going…Heaven is around the bend. It reminds us not to give up or tap out, because the race is worth running.

These are all reasons why we run to cross the finish line. In the words of Angie Gatlin – *"How can we expect to hear well done, when we haven't done well."*

C.H.O.S.E.N.

My final words and the benediction of the Chosen are recorded in 2 Timothy 4:6-8 (NIV):

1. *For I am already being poured out like a drink offering, and the time for my departure is near (v.6).*

2. *I have fought the good fight, I have finished the race, I have kept the faith (v.7).*

3. *Now there is in store for me the crown of righteousness, which the LORD, the righteous Judge (v.8),*

4. *[He] will award to me on that day-and not only to me, but also to all who have longed for his appearing (v. 8).*

Angie M. R. Gatlin

Why Did God Choose Me?

C.H.O.S.E.N.

Angie M. R. Gatlin

C.H.O.S.E.N.

I'm called to...

Angie M. R. Gatlin

C.H.O.S.E.N.

Angie M. R. Gatlin

Personal Reflection...

C.H.O.S.E.N.

Angie M. R. Gatlin

C.H.O.S.E.N.

Hearing God's Voice...

Angie M. R. Gatlin

C.H.O.S.E.N.

Made in the USA
Coppell, TX
01 March 2022